"It's true. When it comes to co-parenting, it's really <u>not</u> complicated."

ALYSHA PRICE

LET ME
SHOW
YOU WHY.

It's Not

PL

TE

A **Self Help Guide** For Mothers Navigating the Obstacles of Co-parenting

Written By: Alysha Price

It's Not Complicated
A Self Help Guide For Mothers Navigating the
Obstacles of Co-parenting
© 2023 by Alysha Price

Published by
The Price Dynamic Inc.
New Hope, MN

All rights reserved. No part of this book may be reproduced in any form or by any means, electronic or mechanical, including photocopying or recording, or by any information storage and retrieval system without written permission of the publisher.

Permission requests should be addressed to:
The Price Dynamic Inc.
4124 Quebec Ave N #209
New Hope, MN 55427

LCCN 2023919034
ISBN 978-1-7339731-2-0

Book Design: Pinkney Creative, LLC.
Cover Photography: Tarin Souriya

Websites:
WWW.ALYSHAPRICE.COM
For Consulting and Speaking Engagements

ACKNOWLEDGMENTS

Organizing my thoughts into this guide has been one of my great accomplishments; however, the one accomplishment that far exceeds anything that I will ever do is giving birth to my son Jasir Tavares Johnson. It is because of his life that I am able to write the words in this guide with such conviction. There is no better joy for me than being his mother.

My son, I thank you for the sparkle I see in your eyes when you look at me, thank you for telling me you are proud of me and most importantly thank you for being such a wonderful child when your father and I were figuring out how to parent you. You hung in there with us like a champ! The cycle will end with you. You will learn from your father and I, as we did our parents. You will create a family of your own that you will be proud of. One where you are the head of your household and a loyal husband to your wife. As your mother, I speak this over your life. I love you to infinity and beyond.

My mother and father, thank you for providing me with an example for which to build my own family upon. You both are amazing individuals but a force when you are together! The ways in which you worked together to instill values, morals and dignity in me is unmatched. You two are the best of both worlds and I am forever grateful for your teachings both intentional and unintentional; I am the woman I am today because of your collective greatness.

ACKNOWLEDGMENTS

My partner in co-parenting, the highest thanks to you my friend! There would be no guide without you… no stories to tell. We absolutely signed up for this journey as we planned our son, he came from love and he is being raised with love. Our ups and downs have strengthened us both and it is my pleasure to have gone on this rollercoaster ride with none other than my friend from the 4th grade. Thank you for your belief and confidence in me; I recall telling you I was thinking of taking this on and you said, "You got this Nik!" You saw this for me and I appreciate you for that.

My keepers, thank you for listening to all my ideas and treating each one as if they were as good as the last even if it wasn't. You all have been my sounding board over the years during my ups and downs as a co-parent; having had my front, back and caught a few people outside with me! Every woman needs an unwavering core group of down ass women to support them (Davenna, April, Antionette, Je'Near, Katoria, and Stacey).

Lastly to my future husband this journey has prepared me for you, I am whole and I am ready.

PREFACE

This is not a guide about fixing the man you have a child with or how to finally get him to do what you've been asking him to do. If that is what you are looking for I can't help you. Chances are you already know that it's impossible to make a person do anything other than what they've decided for themselves. So, let's leave that there and work on YOU! I've created this guide for the mother who understands that she is half of the equation and could stand to take personal inventory of how she became a co-parent and what it takes to build and sustain a cooperative co-parenting partnership. If you are that woman and you're ready to evolve gracefully…I got you! This guide is an invitation to reflect and question your motives, learn steps toward forgiveness, and practice effective communication techniques with the important people in your life.

As a woman I've had my share of uncertain days, heartache, and feelings of being inadequate. Yet, as a mother I needed to maintain my employment and show up sane for my child; there was no time for my hurt feelings. I struggled to keep my emotions in check, similar to a never-ending rollercoaster ride. When the blows from my break up with my son's father knocked me down, I picked up a pen! I wrote down every misunderstanding, argument, fight, and feeling. Writing and reflecting helped me to realize that I had control over all that was happening in my life. Even being cheated on! I could decide to stay or I could take ownership of my role in it all and move on with my self-respect. During my self-inventory I began to see my mother in myself, I could see my father in the man I had chosen. It dawned on me that it was my time to interrupt the cycle. Now, from 16 years of co-parenting and approximately 10 journals filled cover to cover, I bring you "It's Not Complicated" the first of many guides on effective communication.

PREFACE

There is no magic spell or potion that will rid you of the ups and downs brought on by raising a child in the midst of a break up or divorce, hell in the midst of getting to know yourself ...EXPLOSIVE! There is no easy way to get over the pain. You absolutely have to go through it; avoiding it becomes unhealthy and in some cases unsafe. I'm proud to share that I'm on the other side of all the drama. Although, I will not paint a picture that I don't still get triggered. I'm human. However, I have skills and language that help me to keep my son's well-being at the center of my actions. I am not saying what I have written here worked for me so it's guaranteed to work for you. Although what I am saying is that through this guide you will have a heightened awareness of yourself and this is guaranteed to change you for the better.

This guide highlights skills to inspire cooperative co-parenting; however, the skills you learn here can be used to work through many relationships. Before embarking on this journey, you must agree that co-parenting isn't about keeping a relationship with your ex, it's about supporting your child to continue a healthy relationship with their other parent. Co-parenting is an action best shown by parents putting their child's needs first and working together to raise him or her in spite of their failed relationship. You will learn valuable lessons from self-inventory and be encouraged to share what you are learning.

Complicate

com·pli·cate
/kämple,kāt/
verb
verb: complicate; 3rd person present: complicates; past tense: complicated; past participle: complicated; gerund or present participle: complicating
make (something) more difficult or confusing by causing it to be more complex.

TABLE OF CONTENTS

THE CONTENTS

SECTION 1: ALL ABOUT YOU (REFLECTIVE PRACTICE)

- Introspection: Self-Inventory
- Introspection: Get It Out and Carry On
- Foundation: The Core
- Foundation: The Influence
- Foundation: The Woman

SECTION 2: EFFECTIVE LISTENING & SKILL BUILDING

- Skill Building: Forgiveness
- Skill Building: Apologies
- Skill Building: Showing Love
- Skill Building: Standards
- Skill Building: Support System

SECTION 3: COOPERATIVE CO-PARENTING

- Cooperative Co-parenting: Please Can I Co-Parent?
- Cooperative Co-parenting: Be Nice!
- Cooperative Co-parenting: Legal Orders
- Cooperative Co-parenting: Building A Solid Team
- Cooperative Co-parenting: Questions & Hard Answers

SECTION 4: THE PRICE DYNAMIC TOOL KIT

- The Dynamic Four
- Co-Parent Compass
- Cooperative Co-Parent Code of Conduct

ALL ABOUT YOU

Hey CO-PARENTS.

Thank you for allowing me to be your guide on this journey. I am honored that you've welcomed me into your family. I've been where you are right now, trying to decide how much of myself I wanted to give to figuring this co-parenting thing out. Feeling it was unfair that I had to continue to put so much effort into getting along with someone that I wasn't in a relationship with any longer. It can all be overwhelming and there will be times when parenting alone seems easier. But don't you worry I am here with you all the way. I titled this guide, "It's Not Complicated" because once you realize cooperative co-parenting is about your child and not you or your co-parent, it's not complicated! The work you put in becomes necessary. There is no time like the present so let us get started.

INTROSPECTION // SELF-INVENTORY

Self Inventory
ARE YOU READY?

Ready for what you may be asking yourself...ready to create new norms and leave the relationship with your ex behind you. Below I invite you to be honest with yourself, take a moment to see just how ready you truly are to become a mother who is in control of her thoughts, words and actions. Believe it or not you need to ask yourself the hard questions before you're challenged with hard situations. Do not wait or you will suddenly find yourself thinking on your toes and making an ass out of yourself. Having a clear understanding of how ready you are to change and what stage of grief you're in as it relates to the relationship will help you identify ways that you could be holding yourself back. This is the first step in tackling the ambiguous IT'S COMPLICATED stage.

Read the statement below and circle the number that best represents where you currently are as it relates to the statement. (1= Absolutely Not, 5= I Already Do It)

Exercises responsible and respectful behavior in the presence of our child at all times.	1 2 3 4 5
Committed to positive talk about the other parent and his family in the presence of our child.	1 2 3 4 5
Leaves no room for manipulation by the other parent, eliminating the slippery slope (sex).	1 2 3 4 5
Communicates the needs of our child over my own feelings and wants.	1 2 3 4 5
Refrains from inserting my opinion about my ex's new partner unless danger is involved.	1 2 3 4 5
Developed an identity outside of who I was in the relationship with my ex.	1 2 3 4 5

NOW ARE READY FOR THE TRUTH...

ALYSHA PRICE

SCORED 6-15: MS. ACRIMONIOUS

You are in the right place! This guide is going to make you feel like the sinner who hasn't been to church in years and when they finally show up it feels like the sermon is about them! You're thinking will be challenged and you may find out that much of what you believe was learned from women who were very bitter as a result of the same heartache you've experienced. Please do not misunderstand my directness for putting you or the women you love down, that is not it at all. Calling this out is intended to build your awareness of a pathology that has you repeating a cycle. You are going to break the cycle! The more you get to know your "own" thoughts and leave behind the negativity of mislead mothers and hating homegirls you can control your path to successful parenthood. Your challenge is to become more aware of your behaviors, mannerisms, words and craft a positive identity. Stop listening to what others did to get back at or over their ex/child's father and listen to your instinct. Use the reflections and practices in the guide to be brutally honest with yourself and break down your wall.

INTROSPECTION // SELF-INVENTORY

SCORED 16-21:
MS. UNINTENTIONAL

You are in your head a lot, thinking of what's best for your child and trying to be the ultimate mother. Nothing wrong with that right? Only issue is your "I know what's best for my child" campaign keeps you from learning what's best for you. Being still and silent long enough to focus on what's best for you as a mother is not a regular practice of yours. You may connect with feeling as though your child comes first and therefore you don't understand why others can't see your devout motherhood as reason enough to follow your lead. You like to learn and you want to genuinely cooperate for the sake of your child and this guide will give you all the time to think and to test your new learnings. Beware, it will feel very different for you to begin spending some brain power on yourself but, if you pay close attention it will lead to you being a more present mother. Your challenge is to be more spontaneous as it relates to parenting and personal empowerment, everything doesn't need to be by the playbook in your head. Use the reflections and practices in the guide to recognize the good in the, "not so put together," parts of parenting.

SCORED 21-30:
MS. GOODY-GOODY

You have done your work and you feel confident about your parenting; therefore, you are sure this guide isn't for you but for a younger more inexperienced mother. Matter of fact, you have probably purchased this guide as a gift to a friend who you have diagnosed as needing to "GET HER SHIT TOGETHER!" Well Sister, you are not off the hook. You are where I have been several times and until I realized that this parenting thing still had the ability to knock me on my ass I thought I had it mastered too. You will gain so much from taking self-inventory on the little girl inside of you. That little girl still gets her feelings hurt. If you do not fully care for her you will be visiting Ms. Acrimonious the second things don't go your way. Your challenge is to refine your message, be cautious not to come off as judgmental. Help other women by remembering when you were in her shoes. Share your words of wisdom when you can as it will be a form of gratitude. Women that are new to this need women like you in their corner and this guide will remind you of the tender places that tap into your relatability. Your work is never done.

> "I am proud of the woman I am today, feels like I walked through fire to become her."

INTROSPECTION // GOAL GETTER

Self-Inventory GOAL GETTER!

Before you jump in head first take a moment to think about what you hope to get from this guide and how you plan to develop as a cooperative co-parent. Think of clear and attainable goals that are realistic for your current family dynamic. Setting a goal that involves your co-parent may not be wise as you can't guarantee that he shares the same goal. You do not want your success to hinge on someone else's actions. Create M.O.M (measurable, opportune, and motivating) goals and hold yourself accountable for now and no one else.

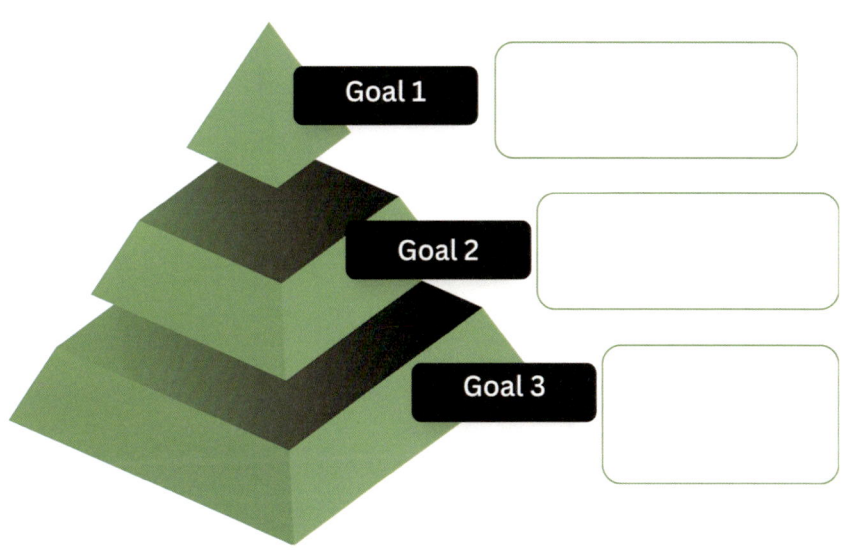

How will you and/or your family situation improve after achieving your goals?

_____
_____
_____
_____

FOUNDATION // THE CORE

The Core
AM I MY PARENTS?

> *"As you develop your co-parenting skill set you will want to reflect on the relationships that you saw as a child, the characteristics of those relationships are embedded in you."*

What lead to your decisions? How did you become a co-parent? It may help you to know that you did not become a co-parent because you chose the wrong person to parent with or because you have commitment issues. How you were raised plays a part in you now labeling yourself a co-parent. As you develop your co-parenting skill set you will want to reflect on the relationships that you saw as a child, the characteristics of those relationships are embedded in you. The relationships you have seen in your lifetime have taught you what to do or don't do, how to be and not be. As you were once an impressionable child whom picked up on the behaviors around you, so is your child!

The first romantic relationship or cohabitation that you saw was likely your parents. Watching them helped to shape your idea of what a healthy or unhealthy relationship looks like. Witnessing your parents also helped to create gender norms, such as, what should a man do and what is a woman's job. I am taking you this far back so you can see how your learned behaviors supported your decision making. In the space provided write out the positives and negatives of both your parents. (If there is another couple you would rather focus on that is perfectly fine, however, note the absence of your parent or parents also informs your mental model about parenting. For example, silence is still communication. Dig deep within to understand how the absence of a parent or parents has helped shape your parenting style.

FOUNDATION // THE CORE

Mother

Father

FOUNDATION // THE INFLUENCE

The Influence
GOING INSIDE

> *"Diving into your past isn't an attempt to label you the same as your parents, the purpose is for you to recognize how their relationship helped shape what you value in your relationships."*

We have all been told at some point that our relationships will mirror what we saw growing up and now that you have had experiences in parenting I am sure you can see your parents in your actions. No matter if your parents were absent they've helped lay the foundation for how you perceive your role as a parent and the expectations you've placed on your co-parent. Science suggests that if you grew up in a stable loving household with both parents you will likely work hard to create that for your children. Luckily, science doesn't work in the reverse…for example you aren't guaranteed to fall in love with a loser just because you never met your father. Diving into your past isn't an attempt to label you the same as your parents, the purpose is for you to recognize how their relationship helped shape what you value in your relationships.

Knowing what you know now, what do you want to pass down to your children? Here's an opportunity to be planful about the qualities and characteristics that you can take from your parents and pass along to your children. Pour into the empty child… Fill him with all the qualities you believe he needs. Write in words that describe what you want to pass along to ensure your children are witnesses to the best part of what your family has to pass down.

FOUNDATION // THE INFLUENCE

17 IT'S NOT COMPLICATED

FOUNDATION // THE WOMAN

The Woman
GIRL, WHO ARE YOU?

> *"The mother in you allows you to make concessions and excuses for people that aren't giving you their all. Although mothers are very protective, we also give our loved ones a lot of room to grow."*

Defining who you are as the mother within your co-parenting unit is imperative although impossible to do if you don't take the time to remember who you are as a woman. The person you were before you became a mother is the woman who will stick to boundaries and will demand self-respect. The mother in you allows you to make concessions and excuses for people that aren't giving you their all. Although mothers are very protective, we also give our loved ones a lot of room to grow. Those passes eventually turn into resentment, my friend! Mom puts on her "super mom" cape and forgets to hang it up sometimes resulting in a worn-out woman. No one wants you to show up as the mother of (insert your child's name) all the time! If you are anything like I was, you sometimes forget to see yourself outside the role of a mother and worse outside of the relationship you once were in with your now co-parent. Here is your permission to reminisce about the dynamic diva inside of you! Resuscitate your sass...

FOUNDATION // THE WOMAN

What are the words you would use to describe the woman you were before motherhood?

_____
_____
_____
_____
_____
_____

Who were the people that helped shape you into the resilient woman you are?

_____
_____
_____
_____
_____
_____

Recall a past experience when you felt ALIVE, the highest level of yourself?

_____
_____
_____
_____
_____
_____

Today, who are you? What changed you?

_____
_____
_____
_____
_____
_____

FOUNDATION // STRAIGHT TALK

Natural High!
STRAIGHT TALK

> *"I will not allow you to make many excuses during your healing process however here you get a pass; rational decisions are tough to make when you are high on chemicals such as dopamine, oxytocin, adrenaline, and vasopressin."*

Let's be honest with ourselves, all children are not conceived in love but, how do you talk about becoming healthy mothers without love? Love can't be absent from this journey. Whether your child was made from a genuine love that eventually faded or a love that was fabricated...love exists! The funny thing about love is we all want it but we are very fickle about giving it. We place an enormous weight on the word by expecting to hear it and searching for ways to earn it, forgetting to look for the actions that prove it.

Think about when you first meet your child's father and that proverbial arrow crashed into your heart. Your brain instantly went on vacation LOL! No really it did, your brain started releasing euphoria-inducing chemicals. According to scientist these chemicals also known as hormones have the same addicting effects on the brain as cocaine. So, I am here to affirm that you were high when you met him. I will not allow you to make many excuses during your healing process however here you get a pass; rational decisions are tough to make when you are high on chemicals such as dopamine, oxytocin, adrenaline, and vasopressin. How were you to know if these wonderful feelings would last a lifetime or be reciprocated.

FOUNDATION // STRAIGHT TALK

"When you come down from that high you begin to see things that the state of euphoria blocked."

Ladies we are so powerful, magical actually! While we are under the influence we craft stories in our mind about our new love, creating an illusion that the man is the perfect fit. When you come down from that high you begin to see things that the state of euphoria blocked. The filters start to fade away allowing you a clearer view of your boo. But how do you contend with what you've told the world?

There is no way to take back the hours you've spent convincing your friends and family how amazing this man is and some of you posted every sacred moment you shared on social media. This is when some of us chose to stay in spite of the conflict between our heart and clear head; ignoring the differing views on commitment, communication, values, success, and dreams.

What did you accept while under the influence that now with a clear mind you will never do again?

_____
_____
_____
_____
_____
_____
_____
_____
_____
_____
_____
_____

Effective Listening
SKI
BUI
DIN

"Take control, this is your time to create a new narrative"

FORGIVENESS. THE UNLEARNED SKILL.

ALYSHA PRICE

Any process exploring forgiveness of others must start with you. Forgiving yourself is the most important part of forgiveness. Stop punishing yourself for mistakes you've made. Unconsciously you are punishing your co-parent and child too. As half of the co-parenting unit you are working to build or solidify you must own that you are half of the reason you are in this situation. It doesn't matter how much he may have done…you chose him! Say that aloud for me, I CHOSE HIM. That might be a hard pill to swallow but it's your pill. It's necessary to hold yourself accountable in order to move forward. Put on your big girl drawers and get on with the rest of your life. You may need to forgive yourself for the role you played in the demise of the relationship or for becoming intimate with someone who you didn't know well enough to make a parent. Take a moment to reflect on your regrets. Begin telling your truth.

SKILL BUILDING // FORGIVENESS

To forgive myself I must admit that I could have done this differently... (what did I do that now I realize wasn't the right course of action?)

_____
_____
_____
_____
_____
_____
_____
_____

To forgive myself I must admit that I ignored...(what did you ignore although your best judgement told you not to?)

_____
_____
_____
_____
_____
_____
_____
_____

Now that you have done the pre-work you should be ready to cut yourself some slack. You now have an awareness of why you are here; remove the blame and begin taking ownership of your individual role and responsibility. **Never forget it takes two!**

"If you feel shame, fear, or guilt, it was wrong."
– Mr. Floyd, My Father

SKILL BUILDING // FORGIVENESS

UNFORGIVENESS

Unforgiveness is the biggest piece of baggage that you can carry. Your baggage could be from a parent, friend, significant other, or coworker— anyone that was not there for you, abused you, took advantage of your trust, or harmed you emotionally.

What FORGIVENESS really is...	What FORGIVENESS will never be...
Webster's Dictionary definition of **FORGIVENESS** *"To give up resentment against; stop being angry with; pardon; give up all claim to punish; overlook; cancel a debt."* *In other word's forgiveness is letting go of the feeling that he owes you something.*	Reconciliation with the person.
	Denial about what his action(s) and pretending certain things ever took place.
	Accepting the same behavior over and over again.
	No consequence for disrespecting you.

SKILL BUILDING // FORGIVENESS

Forgiving My CO-PARENT

The second step to forgiveness is to give your co-parent the same gift you just gave yourself. Nursing resentment toward your co-parent creates barriers between you. It makes true vulnerability impossible and models the wrong behavior to your children. This blocks the positivity that you desire from flowing to you and from you. Most importantly, holding onto resentment for wrongdoings in your past relationship will not undo the experience therefore the pain of it remains in the present. Give yourself permission to let it go now. Release yourself and your partner from the pain of holding onto it.

One thing I would like to release myself from and forgive my co-parent for is?

_____
_____
_____
_____
_____

What do you expect him to say or do that would make it possible for you to genuinely forgive him?

_____
_____
_____
_____

SKILL BUILDING // FORGIVENESS

Road to
FORGIVENESS

STAGE OF CHANGE:

1. THINK ABOUT IT: Precontemplation
2. TALK ABOUT IT: Contemplation
3. PRACTICE IT: Preparation
4. SHOW HIM: Action
5. KEEP THE SAME ENERGY: Maintenance
6. DON'T BRING IT UP AGAIN: Termination

SKILL BUILDING // FORGIVENESS

Mapping FORGIVENESS

1. THINK ABOUT IT: Compile a "forgiveness list" of events/behaviors/actions of your co-parent you need to forgive. Get it all out.

_____
_____
_____
_____
_____
_____

2. TALK ABOUT IT: Admit how your unwillingness to forgive has caused you pain. How is the memory more painful than the actual series of events?

_____
_____
_____
_____
_____
_____

3. PRACTICE IT: If there are items on your forgiveness list that you have never addressed with the person, get in a mirror and go for it. Have the courage to say it alone and not be attached to the outcome. [If you laugh while practicing mark that one off your forgiveness list. Pick your battles chile! Everything doesn't need to be addressed.]

_____
_____
_____
_____
_____

SKILL BUILDING // FORGIVENESS

> *"You are responsible for doing what's best for you and this can mean cutting ties with your ex."*

4. SHOW HIM: Without an apology, you must express that you have forgiven him for the actions that you found to be most important on your list. Find the most comfortable way to take action; write a letter, send an email or text, speak in-person or over the phone.

_____
_____
_____
_____
_____

5. KEEP THAT ENERGY: Be consistent, don't go back on your word. Once you've said you forgive you must mean it. Release your expectations of apologies and improvement to behavior. Forgiving doesn't mean accepting disrespectful behavior. You are responsible for doing what's best for you and this can mean cutting ties with your ex. How do you hold yourself accountable to being consistent?

_____
_____
_____
_____
_____

6. DON'T BRING IT UP AGAIN: Feelings of hurt can creep back up, this is normal. Write down what you think may trigger you. How will you redirect yourself?

_____
_____
_____
_____
_____

SKILL BUILDING // APOLOGIES

Apologies
SORRY DOESN'T MAKE IT RIGHT

> *"Never say you're sorry, you're not a sorry person... Say you apologize."*
> -Velma Nelson Thomas, My Mother

Sis, I am aware that if he tells you he's sorry, the sorry isn't enough if you are still hurt! Over time you have developed expectations about what a meaningful apology feels like; understand that this is unrealistic as apologies do not erase feelings. His apology may very well be sincere but if your wounds are still raw you will not receive it. Sure, some things happened that hurt you; you deserve an apology and you are still responsible for how you feel. The key to accepting an apology is knowing that apologies don't come when you need them. In order to accept an apology, you must be able to recognize an apology. While this seems simple it's one of the most difficult skills to master as a co-parent and like anything else you want to be good at it, it takes practice. You will know that you have concurred the hurt when you can separate your feelings from fault. When you are able to immediately recognize that no matter who is at fault for the experience, you are responsible for how you feel about it. To arrive at this place is to no longer be tied to an apology.

RECOGNIZING APOLOGIES
Did you know there are different types of apologies? There can't be a one size fits all apology because they are so many ways to cause pain. Depending on your experience you may be listening for your co-parent to right his wrong by verbalizing regret or own up to what he did.

SKILL BUILDING // APOLOGIES

Look for your co-parent in the chart below, see if you recognize the way he typically apologizes. **Check the apology type/statement that is closest to what you recognize in him.**

APOLOGY TYPE	APOLOGY STATEMENT
MR. RESPITE He asks you for forgiveness and by doing this is showing that he understands what he did. He holds forgiveness as a value and may have the ability to teach this to your children.	*"Will you please forgive me?"* *"Are you going to forgive me?"* *"I need your forgiveness."* ☐
MR. REGRETFUL He shows he is aware of what he did to hurt you and acknowledges your pain. He is willing to express vulnerability with you (exposing his heart). He may look for your children to be able to be emotionally expressive.	*"If I could do it over again I Would never _____."* *"I am very sorry for_____."* *"I see how I have hurt you."* ☐
MR. RESPONSIBLE He openly admits to his wrongdoing and takes ownership. He can state if he made a mistake and doesn't feel less than a man for doing so. He may hold your children accountable for their mistakes.	*"I was wrong."* *"I am wrong."* *"There is no excuse for what I did."* ☐
MR. RECONCILE He knows you love him and values reconciling the relationship. He is searching for the silver lining. He may pass his charm on to your children.	*"What can I do to make it right?"* *"Look what I bought you!"* *"I will do whatever you ask."* ☐

SKILL BUILDING // APOLOGIES

Next, it's your turn to identify the type of apology that you connect most with, put a check mark in the box. ***Does his apology type align with the way you want to receive an apology?***

APOLOGY PREFERENCE	APOLOGY RESULTS	
A) You need him to articulate that he understands what he did to <u>hurt</u> you, a heart-felt apology fulfills your expectations.	His Apology Type:_____ My Apology Preference:_____	
B) You need him to <u>show</u> that he wants to be forgiven and is willing to admit fault. You are looking for facial expressions to determine his authenticity.	What are the positives about how he apologizes? 1. 2.	How can you help him learn your preference? 1. 2.
C) You feel as though he has wronged you yet you feel able to forgive if he makes you <u>an</u> offer. The length he is willing to go to get out of the dog house determines his sincerity to you.	3. 4. 5.	3. 4 5.
D) You need to hear that he is keeping it real. You need to hear him say exactly what he did. The <u>truth</u> is somewhere between the admitting and responsibility for you.		

Let's be REALISTIC.

It is not necessary for his style and your preference to be aligned; however, you can take this information and use it to help recognize when he is truly working toward your forgiveness. Being honest about your preference will help you to be realistic with your expectations. Looking for a gift from your co-parent who is now in a new relationship doesn't exactly seem possible, so if you are waiting for this you will likely never feel like he has apologized.

Tip: Use this in new relationships. When you are building with someone and taking time to get to know them this information can be useful. Men don't enjoy guessing, the more information that we can arm them with the better. Chances are a man that knows how you prefer to receive an apology will follow this strategy. Thus, resulting in you feeling heard and the both of your finding a common ground sooner.

SKILL BUILDING // APOLOGIES

In 100 words or less draft the apology you believe you deserve from your co-parent...Use the apology preference that you selected from the previous exercise. The word limit is designed to make sure you focus and get straight to the point.

_____
_____
_____
_____
_____
_____
_____
_____
_____
_____
_____
_____
_____
_____
_____
_____
_____
_____
_____
_____
_____
_____

Now that you have gotten that off of your chest... Let it go! Release the attachment to an apology that you may never receive. Take control, this is your time to create a new narrative. Instead of mourning an apology that only you may believe you deserve you can now be proud that you are the operator of the rollercoaster and no one else.

SKILL BUILDING // APOLOGIES

What do you expect him to say or do that would make it possible for you to genuinely forgive him?

_____
_____
_____
_____
_____
_____
_____
_____
_____
_____
_____
_____
_____
_____
_____
_____
_____
_____
_____
_____
_____
_____
_____
_____
_____

Tip: Apologize in person, when possible, face to face communication removes any question that the apology is not sincere. Consider whether an audience is necessary, some people appreciate witnesses because they feel as though they were publicly hurt therefore a public apology is vindicating.

SKILL BUILDING // SHOWING LOVE

Love HEART RATE

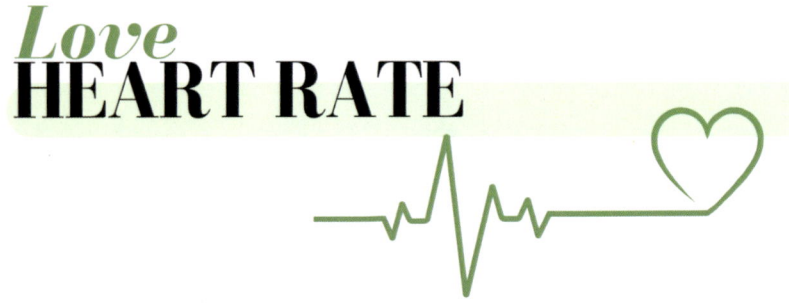

"Worrying less about what your counterpart is doing and focusing more on what you have to give."

Measure the love you give. The best thing you can do to improve your co-parent relationship is to improve your contribution to the partnership. The way to improve that is to measure what you are contributing. Worrying less about what your counterpart is doing and focusing more on what you have to give. Fill the heart on the next page with all the ways that you see yourself giving to the partnership. This can be, everything from Father's Day gifts to a simple thank you... it all counts. As you watch the heart fill up recognize what you tend to focus most on. Where is there room for improvement as it pertains to your willingness to show love, appreciation, and kindness toward your co-parent. Note, if your heart is empty you may need to do some foundational work on the relationship and in this case brainstorm ways you can begin to show your co-parent a kinder side of you. Do not rush to fill the heart in one setting, it's absolutely alright to take your time to let the heart beat build.

SKILL BUILDING // SHOWING LOVE

Wow! Your Child Must Be Proud!

THAT A Girl!

GREAT Progress!

INCREASE Your Effort!

SKILL BUILDING // STANDARDS

Standards NON-NEGOTIABLES

"Setting non-negotiables is very different than telling someone what you don't like or what you wish they would do."

Forgiving and apologizing are all essential to your success as a co-parent and so is having standards. I like to call those standards the "Non-Negotiables." Think about non-negotiables as deal breakers if you will; these are things you are under no circumstances willing to accept. Notice I say "willing," there is indeed a difference between being able to accept something and to be willing. I am able to jump rope in the middle of the street but am I willing to? NO!

The truth is before you enter into any relationship you should consider what you absolutely can't do without and what you will not deal with. This goes for everything from intimate relationships to employers. Knowing your terms and having the confidence to state them helps others know how to treat you and it also helps you permeate the respect you have for yourself. Us women know how to articulate what we do not want; matter of fact we spit the do not list out with quickness. Yet when we are asked what do we want there is a big question mark hovering over our heads at times. Setting non-negotiables is very different than telling someone what you don't like or what you wish they would do. This is you defining the actions and traits you will and will not be willing to accept in your co-parenting relationship. But let me be clear, this list is not permission to exile the father of your child from your life if he pushes your buttons or the boundaries of your list. This exercise is meant to help you get clear in advance. Stretch yourself, your able list should have some things that you compromise on and your unwilling list should have things that as mentioned above are non-negotiable.

SKILL BUILDING // STANDARDS

For Example, I was able to pick my son up from his father's girlfriend's house. At the time it wasn't something I wanted to do but I was able to do that so my son could spend time with his father. This was one of those times when I had to put my feelings aside and think about my son having a relationship with his father. However, I was unwilling to have my son in the home if people were smoking cigarettes. That was non-negotiable for me. Once I was clear on this with myself I was able to explain my concerns without it turning into an argument. Pervious to my clarity I would mention something like this and my son's father would take it to mean I was trying to control him rather than advocate for what I believed to be best for our child. Thank god he was rationale and in the long run felt the same about protecting our child from second-hand smoke.

Use the chart below to write out your list...

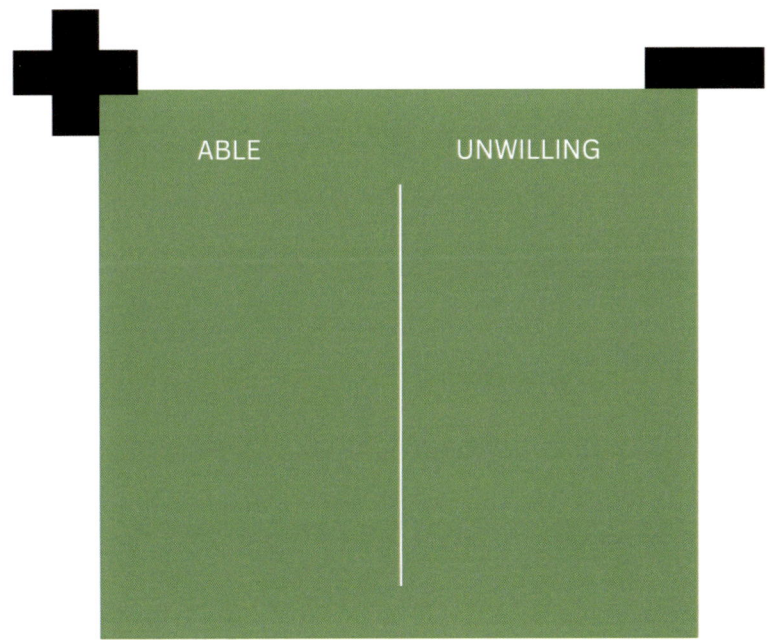

ABLE	UNWILLING

SKILL BUILDING // STANDARDS

Now, review your unwilling list and make a commitment to yourself to never go back on your word. Reminder…this list is for your eyes only so be completely honest with yourself. If you absolutely cannot and will not stand for something, draw a line and stick to it. This isn't a wish list, this is a "don't try me" list.

Time for practice, **write out** what you will say to your co-parent about your non-negotiable list. How will you present your non-negotiables in a respectful way?

_____
_____
_____
_____
_____
_____
_____
_____
_____
_____
_____
_____
_____
_____
_____
_____
_____

Tip: Your list must not have phrases in it like, "You should," or "You better not." These are not positive ways to begin asking someone to comply or follow your lead on something. The conversation will go over much better if you keep a neutral stance saying, "There are a few things I want to get your thoughts on that I see as imperative to our child's safety and success."

SUPPORT SYSTEM. STARTING LINE UP.

ALYSHA PRICE

When your co-parent crosses the line, doesn't follow through or just plain old pisses you off, who do you turn to? This is a tough one. You deserve to release these feelings just as much as you deserve to not be repeatedly disappointed. The frustration that comes from your co-parent's actions can seem more stress-inducing than any other relationship you have. You can manage this stress by managing your expectations; however, that doesn't necessarily relieve you of those, "I'm irritated right now feelings." We've already established that you and I have some things in common so I am willing to bet that you vent to your closest friends or seek the advice of your mother. Caution! I want to encourage you to think before you vent or solicit advice from just any old friend or family member. In the famous words of Maya Angelou, "Words are things." You can't take back what you say and if your words are venomous that poison will come back to infect you. Have you ever told a friend something and she later asks you about it when you are over it or simply don't care to talk about it anymore? Whoops!

SKILL BUILDING // SUPPORT SYSTEM

> *"Understanding how your friends contribute to your evolution is key to the longevity of the relationship."*

Every woman should have a starting line up! Here's why...
When you are upset with your co-parent your instinct is to take control, in other words trying to score – win! You become most focused on getting the result you'd hoped for and if or when you realize that isn't going to happen, let the games begin. I've been there done that and girl let me tell you all of this can be exhausting! When running offense you need defense. Have you figured it out yet? The role of your starting line-up is to play defense! They prevent the other team from trying to score; you no longer have to work so hard for the win!

We look for our family and friends to be our sounding board, comfort, and to give us valuable feedback. However, when you are dealing with something as critical as parenting and creating a healthy foundation for your child, you cannot trust just anyone to have the skills to equip you with reasonable support. A person can only offer you what they know based on their personal experience or learnings. So how do you consult with your friend who has failed relationships or your mother who may stress that you don't need a man to help you raise your child. The key to building a strong support system is knowing which person is best equip to inform, guide you or just listen without judgement. Studies show that people have much better friendships when they know what exactly to go to each friend for. Understanding how your friends contribute to your evolution is key to the longevity of the relationship. The title friend has lost its level of importance, we can thank social media for this. With Facebook, Twitter, and Snapchat just to name a few; our small circle of "friends" grows to hundreds/thousands of "friends" following our lives.

However, the influence or advice of those far away "friends" may not be what's best for you. Now let's develop your line up!

SKILL BUILDING // SUPPORT SYSTEM

Starting Line Up **CHART**

STARTING LINE UP	SQUAD
"The Rational" Voice of Reason- Helps to calm you down and has the ability to see the point of view of all parties involved.	
"The Rider" Down for Whatever- Willing to match your energy, this friend is courageous and willing to stand up for you.	
"The Resourceful" Business-Minded- Can connect you to information and/or professionals that can help you deal with the matter at hand.	
"The Reinforcement" Reminder-The person that will hold you accountable and recall all the ways that you said you would improve. When you think of back sliding this friend steps in.	
"The Realist" Calls It Out-Tells you the things that you may not want to hear but need to hear. This friend isn't afraid to hurt your feelings for the greater good.	
"The Responder" Wordsmith-Helps you find the right words to send in text, email or in a real-time conversation, has a knack for helping you say things in a classy yet direct manner.	

"I call my starting line up my keepers, we don't talk every day but we'll ride for each other any day." **-Alysha Price**

COOPERATIVE

Co Parenting

> Relationships may have expiration dates but the work of a parent doesn't expire.

CC// PLEASE CAN I CO-PARENT?

Co-Parenting
PLEASE, CAN I CO-PARENT?

Just think if you had to ask permission to be a parent to your child! The very thought of that seems strange, right? In my experience coaching fathers who are working at being cooperative co-parents, I've learned that many of them feel as though they have to ask for permission to be a father to their children. These men feel judged and belittled. While I understand there are two sides to every story, the reality is as mothers we tend to protect our children to the point of controlling the other parent.

Do the following questions sound familiar?

Where are you taking MY child?
Who's going to be there?
What will you be doing?
When are you coming back?
Why can't you visit at another time?

These are not bad questions, as a matter of fact, they are great questions for a person you do not trust. Think about that for a second. Do you trust the father of your child? In some cases there are very good reasons not to trust people based on their actions however, I will assume (which I rarely do) that if you are reading this guide on how to make your co-parenting relationship less complicated, you generally trust the father and want him to be in your child's life. If you are questioning some of his actions and or who he has around your child it is necessary you address those issues. However, addressing your concerns is not the same as questioning him.

One of the most universal questions of all parents trying to cooperatively co-parent is,
"Who is going to be around my child?"

Co-Parenting
BE NICE

> *"Men aren't as straightforward as we women tend to be and the last thing you want to hear when you are trying to BE SERIOUS is BE NICE!"*

Becoming a cooperative co-parent isn't something that happens overnight. As you know it takes work to remove your personal feelings and begin to see the person as a parent not an ex! This can be a difficult transition for some as co-parenting success hinges on each parent's ability to reciprocate positive behavior. In order to have a successful co-parenting relationship you must be willing to nurture it just as you do any other relationship in your life. All relationships in your life require patience, empathy and communication. All of this sounds like common sense, right? Well, not so much! When emotions get in the way, common sense can escape us.

In my experience men like to say, "Be Nice," this seemingly kind ask once irritated the crap out of me. After some thought I realized that all they were trying to say is, "Don't do that thing that you are doing." Men aren't as straightforward as we women tend to be and the last thing you want to hear when you are trying to BE SERIOUS is BE NICE! I have taken the liberty of creating a short list of eight do not's. I believe if you use these as a guide for communicating you will be consistent and therefore easier to predict and get along with.

COOPERATIVE COPARENTING// BE NICE

The DO NOT List

- **Do not** reframe the question you are being asked. "So, what you are saying is..."
- **Do not** withhold the answer if you know it.
- **Do not** insist that your co-parent answer their own question first. "I'll answer after you tell me your answer."
- **Do not** ask questions you already know the answer to.
- **Do not** assume that any time is the best time to talk about family matters.
- **Do not** withhold information about school events or Dr. appointments.
- **Do not** try to be more than Co-parents... NO Co-parents with benefits!
- **Do not** reserve your communication for the only bad things.

To learn more about The Price Dynamic approach visit www.thepricedynamic.com

> "Don't be difficult it's interpreted as bitter."

COOPERATIVE COPARENTING// LEGAL ORDERS

Co-Parenting **LEGAL ORDERS**

The Price Dynamic approach is to support families to establish a co-parenting relationship without having to involve the courts; building up the courage to stay committed when it gets tough but understanding that the courts do not love your child so how can they truly know what's best for you. However, I understand that at times that is not possible and having legal representation and or legal agreements to assist in establishing healthy parenting practices can be helpful. I encourage you to do what is best for your family in the long term not short term. Sometimes short-term solutions don't align with how you feel once you've calmed down and your emotions aren't so intense, this can cause long term implications. Should you and your co-parent be legally separated or divorced, you most likely have set guidelines established by a court on how to maintain the safety and welfare of your child. If you have not yet involved the courts let's review what common court orders typically address.

LEGAL CUSTODY	**PHYSICAL CUSTODY**	**PARENTING TIME**
Determines if both parents will be accountable for decisions regarding education, health care, and other essentials affecting your childs well-being. This can be sole custody or joint custody.	Establishing where a child will live. In cases of joint physical custody, this means a child lives with both parents, at established times.	Determined when parents share physical custody or if one has visitation, a parent's right to see their child is scheduled for specific times.

IT'S NOT COMPLICATED

COOPERATIVE COPARENTING// LEGAL ORDERS

How Does THE COURT MAKE CUSTODY DECISIONS?

Typically, courts make custody decisions based on what's in the best interest of the child. However, parents that can come to a reasonable agreement before going to court are generally supported and awarded what they have agreed upon. The following areas are likely to be considered in establishing custody:

INPUT FROM THE CHILD
Courts often take into consideration what the child is experiencing based on their own account if they are older.

HOW WELL THE PARENTS GET ALONG WITH EACH OTHER
Parents who are civil and can show a willingness to co-parent often are awarded joint custody.

PARENTS ABILITY TO ENSURE A SAFE AND STABLE ENVIRONMENT
A parent who is abusive, shows signs of alcohol or drug abuse, and is homeless or highly mobile is not seen as fit to provide a safe and stable environment.

COOPERATIVE COPARENTING// BUILDING A SOLID TEAM

Co-Parenting
BUILDING A SOLID TEAM

> *"Your children need stability in housing and in your decision making. Therefore, getting on the same page is imperative to your success."*

If we are being real with ourselves—Co-parenting is challenging! Your family structure requires a different type of action now. Ideas about discipline, education, and family norms may be challenged as you are no longer in the same household to work these things out in real-time. While this is your new normal, your children need stability in housing and in your decision-making. Therefore, getting on the same page is imperative to your success. Establishing a written parenting agreement can serve as a map that keeps your family on track. Produce a parenting agreement that works for your children and you as co-parents.

Establishing a "Winning Team"
To create an effective co-parenting team, you and your co-parent must agree to AGREE! This means getting on the same page (sharing a mutual interest) and putting your personal feelings aside. These are the characteristics of a winning team:

- Sharing responsibilities and duties.
- Communicate directly and respectfully.
- Never speaking ill about the other parent in the presence of the child.
- Settle disagreements in a timely manner, not holding a grudge.
- Maintain a routine for the child and stick to it.

COOPERATIVE COPARENTING// BUILDING A SOLID TEAM

PARENTING AGREEMENT DETAILS

Once you've agreed that taking a team approach to parenting is best you can then move on to creating your plan to hold yourselves accountable. A written parenting agreement is like a coach's play book, now let's explore the plays that will lead you to victory!

Every parenting agreement should have the following:

- **Living Arrangements**- Detailing which parent the child will stay with and on which days. It is also good to plan ahead for holidays as you discuss living arrangements.

- **Expenses-** Spell out how you will share the cost associated with the care of your child. This reviews everyday needs, mental/dental, and enrichment activities such as music lessons, sports, or tutoring.

- **Education-** Where your child will go to school and transportation to and from school is a huge part of any parenting agreement. Additionally, having a plan for how homework will be supported and who will attend parent-teacher conferences.

- **Discipline-** Clearly articulate how rules will be set and what the consequences are for breaking rules. This should be appropriate for the child's age and needs to be revisited as the child matures.

While these are not all the areas covered in a parenting agreement these will get any co-parenting team started on the right path. If you are seeking more help and guidance on developing a parent agreement also known as a parenting plan you can reach out to The Price Dynamic or any other mediation service to assist you in creating a plan that works for your family.

COOPERATIVE COPARENTING// PARENTING STYLES

Co-Parenting PARENTING STYLES

Co-parents are no different than married parents in the sense that we all want the best for our children. We also have to figure out the best way to achieve that goal. But how exactly do you reach that goal? Establishing a shared style of parenting is a great first step. The consistency that comes from sharing a parenting style helps to develop a well-adapted child. There are several decisions you will have to make together so aligning yourselves will help create a solid foundation for co-parenting.

First step in establishing a shared parenting style is discussing each other's values, principles and beliefs about child rearing. Having a major difference of opinion in the following areas will no doubt divide you. Values, principles and beliefs help to build parenting strategies. You will use these discussions to come to agreement on the following:

- How to discipline and what rules to set
- Creating a routine for such things as bed time, homework, eating dinner, etc.
- Chores to be divided across households
- How to handle financial expenses

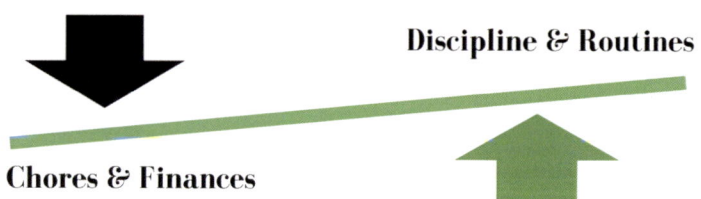

You can have opposing views and opinions however cooperative co-parenting is about finding a sweet balance between your preferences and his. You both will have experiences and learnings to bring to the table that will make you unique as individual parents, combining those things is what gives your child a sense that you all are a true team.

CC// QUESTIONS & HARD TRUTHS

Co-Parenting
QUESTIONS & HARD TRUTHS

Q: Can I decide not to allow my child's father to see our child because I don't want to see him?

A: No, he has the right to see his child. Generally, it is ideal for a child to spend time with his or her father. The father's circumstance may dictate whether or not visitation is possible and the regularity of the visits. However, mothers do not have the right to keep their child from his or her father. The role of mother doesn't give you permission to say no to visits.

Q: If I earn more money than my child's father will he still have to pay child support?

A: Yes, all non-custodial parents have the obligation of financially supporting their children based on their ability. Note, based on ability; this means the amount may not be what you desire. If paternity is not established, child support can't be ordered by a court.

Q: If I never married my child's father how does he establish his rights as a father?

A: Most states have a form called the Recognition of Parentage, Declaration of Parentage, or Voluntary Paternity Acknowledgment form (the name of this form varies from state to state). This form is usually presented while you are still in the hospital after giving birth. If the father is present he has the opportunity to sign stating he agrees he is the father or the child and accepts responsibility. If he later finds out he is not the father he will need to get this revoked by sending a letter to the states department of Health.

CC// QUESTIONS & HARD TRUTHS

Q: How can I prove that I am using child support payments to care for my child?

A: Consistently provide safe and secure housing, adequate meals, proper clothing, and access to high quality education. Putting your child's needs at the forefront of your to do list every day. This doesn't mean that you shouldn't treat yourself to nice things however your child's needs should never be comprised for your wants. Keep record of purchases for tax purposes such as daycare, after school programs, etc.

Q: If I don't really know my child's father what are the types of things I should talk to him about?

A: For starters getting to know the person you are parenting with is critical not only to building a successful co-parenting relationship but in understanding your child's characteristics and genetics. Asking about his family's medical history as well as his, can help you be proactive about your child's health. Should your child ever need an organ transplant you would need to know this type of information. You may also want to find out what type of student he was and what his values are about education. Inquire about his hobbies, these may turn out to be talents that your child will display later in life.

Q: My child's father brings new women around my child too often how do I stop this behavior?

A: You can't stop this if you want your child to have a relationship with his or her father. You will not approve of everyone that he has in his life and you have no way of knowing if the relationships will become serious and long-term. What you can focus on is expressing your concerns in a healthy way so that he can receive your concerns and take them into consideration.

THE PRICE DYNAMIC TOOL KIT// CODE OF CONDUCT
Notes

Building
COM[M
NIC[A
TIO[

The Price Dynamic Tool Kit

THE PRICE DYNAMIC TOOL KIT// THE DYNAMIC FOUR

Cooperative CO-PARENT

BE RESPECTFUL

BE AUTHENTIC

BE INTERESTED

BE VULNERABLE

THE DYNAMIC FOUR

BE VULNERABLE	Share your emotions and needs
BE AUTHENTIC	Natural interactions only, don't fake friendly
BE RESPECTFUL	Eliminate Drama, Show care and concern
BE INTERESTED	Ask Questions and listen in new ways

"A vulnerable woman feels deeply and loves endlessly, doesn't hide her tears, and is both tender and strong. A vulnerable woman in her essence is a mother...tougher than all." -Alysha Price

THE PRICE DYNAMIC TOOL KIT// CO-PARENT COMPASS

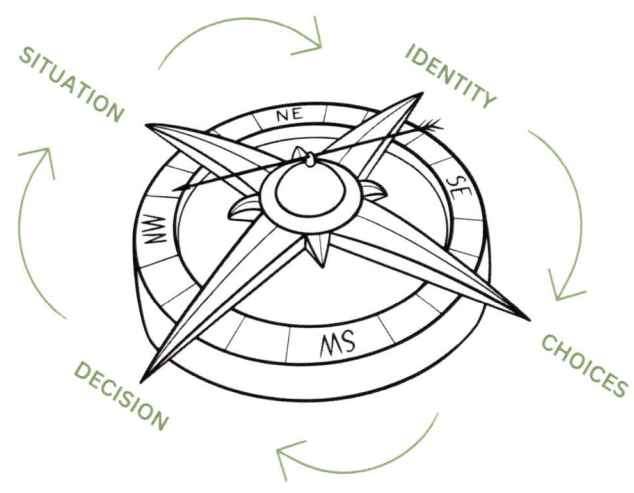

Co-Parent COMPASS

- **SITUATION:** External Examination, thoroughly thinking through what has occurred that requires you to interact with your co-parent. Dig deep, sometimes what is on the surface may not be the real situation.
- **IDENTITY:** Internal Examination, here is where you determine the lens in which you use to respond. This area is critical, will you be the hurt ex, the protective mother or will you be the co-parent trying to work things out?
- **CHOICES:** Evaluate your options, this is the time to recognize that you are not powerless, you actually have the choice to act positively or react negatively toward your co-parent. A person with options is limitless.
- **DECISION:** This you can not change! Whatever you decide is permanent therefore you will want to be mindful of the pervious directions on your compass. Your final decision is one you will want to be good living with.

THE PRICE DYNAMIC TOOL KIT// CODE OF CONDUCT

Co-Parent
CODE OF CONDUCT

I/We Solemnly swear to reiterate my/our commitment to conduct my/our family business in a manner that benefits the well-being of ____Insert Childs Name____ and our continued growth as a co-parenting family. I will exercise empathy and respect at all times when I feel frustrated. I will approach my concerns with a tolerant and accommodating nature and uphold our family value that ____Insert Childs Name____ deserves a parent/parents who act with self-dignity.

I/We hereby commit to abide by the Code of Conduct for Cooperative Co-parenting, recognizing that ____Insert Childs Name____ is fragile and learning from my/ our actions. I/We further pledge that providing the best home environments and safety is an essential ingredient to the proper development of ____Insert Childs Name____ and therefore I/ We will not have individuals around whose actions are in direct conflict with this.

I/We support open communication and therefore encourage ____Insert Childs Name____ to express how he/she is feeling. Open communication will be met with an open mind recognizing that ____Insert Childs Name____ views and opinions are critical indicators of success.

Signature_____
Date _____
On behalf of_____
In the presence of_____

Notes

Notes

www.ingramcontent.com/pod-product-compliance
Lightning Source LLC
Chambersburg PA
CBRC091725070526
44585CB00011B/179